Designer Hotels

Designer

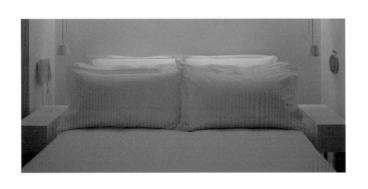

Hotels

Publisher: **Paco Asensio**   Editor and introductory text: **Aurora Cuito**   Texts: **Alejandro Bahamón**   Translation: **Wendy Griswold**   Art Director: **Mireia Casanovas Soley**   Graphic Design & layout: **Emma Termes Parera**   2001 © **LOFT** Publications   Domènech, 7-9 2º 2ª 08012 Barcelona. España   Phone: **+34 93 218 30 99**   Fax: **+34 93 237 00 60** loft@loftpublications.com   www.loftpublications.com   Hardcover ISBN: **0-06-621362-2**   Paperback ISBN: **0-8230-1301-4**   D.L.: **B-47.365-01**   2001 ©   First published in 2001 by LOFT and HBI, an imprint of HarperCollins Publishers 10 East 53rd St. New York, NY 10022-5299 Distributed in the U.S. and Canada by Watson-Guptill Publications 770 Broadway New York, NY 10003-9595 Ph.: (800) 451-1741 or (732) 363-4511 in NJ, AK, HI Fax: (732) 363-0338 Distributed throughout the rest of the world by HarperCollins International 10 East 53rd St. New York, NY 10022-5299 Fax: (212) 207-7654

Suite Dreams

Although most people consider the home the place where they get the best night's sleep, people who have stayed at the hotels in this book might disagree.

After an exhausting business trip or a long day of shopping, true pleasure is not at home sweet home, but in an impeccable room where a basket of fruit and a bottle of champagne, a soft bathrobe, and a new bar of perfumed soap await you.

You can log onto the internet, videoconference with your loved ones, or miss them while relaxing in the Jacuzzi. You can sit on a sofa by Antonio Citterio, next to a Phillipe Starck stool, by the light of an Ingo Maurer lamp.

You are surrounded by attractive materials (trimmed marble, exotic woods, or multicolored fabrics), fine finishes (galvanized metals, lacquered walls, and acid-etched glass), and construction details precise down to the last millimeter, so you can experience new sensations and your comfort will be not just physical, but emotional, almost spiritual.

Who wants to feel at home, when you can feel as though you're in the home you've always dreamed of?

EUROPE

The 204 rooms of Saint Martin's Lane enjoy an exceptional location in bustling Covent Garden. Ian Schrager chose London as the first European city to which he would venture because it has become the world center of pop culture, home to the latest trends in fashion, architecture, design, music, and theater.

The project's goal was to experiment, cross perceptive frontiers, build a new paradigm that would reconsider the essence of symbolism, and reinterpret the idea of the hotel as theater, already exploited in the chain's other establishments. The settings were conceived as flexible spaces that would be more than just a place to sleep, reinventing the idea of accommodation for the select clientele.

Having collaborated with him in other cities, Ian Schrager again relied on the eccentric and brilliant Philippe Starck, whose method is based on developing projects so unique and magical that they transcend design and celebrate exuberant creativity and humor. The result is a collision of influences, a hotel that breaks the rules, based on diversity, a place where fashion is rejected to create a modern benchmark of originality.

The lobby is the meeting place, the social center, the village where the hotel's six public spaces (two bars, two restaurants, a café, and a film library) come together. The reception area, which is entered through tall revolving glass doors, consists of an irregularly-shaped space with some spots painted an almost-fluorescent yellow, furnished with original pieces. Noteworthy among these are stools by Starck himself.

The rooms are very comfortable and incorporate the latest in interactive art. An advanced lighting system allows guests to choose the color of the light according to their mood. The enormous windows looking out on the street bring this play of colors outside to create a changing façade like a luminous mosaic.

Saint
Martin's
Lane

The Sea bar was inspired by Japanese fish markets and offers a wide variety of shellfish and sushi. The counter is white marble imported from Yugoslavia. Above the counter, food is displayed on a mountain of ice. The Louis XVI-style chairs have aluminum frames and are topped with white fabric cushions.

Designer: **Philippe Starck**   Photographer: **Todd Eberle**   Address: **45 St Martin's Lane, London, United Kingdom**   Tel.: **44 204 200 55 00**   Fax: **44 207 300 55 01**

Opening date: **September 1999**   Number of rooms: **204**   Services: **two restaurants, two bars, gym, meeting room, newsstand, gift shop, theater, data ports**

With the invaluable assistance of Robert De Niro, a film library has been set up. It will house several projection rooms, a specialized library, and a bar. It's the perfect place for taking in independent film premieres and director film festivals.

The Asia de Cuba Restaurant is the domain of Jeffrey Chodorow, the famous chef who combines Latin and Asian cuisine to create deliciously original dishes. The majestic columns throughout the restaurant help create a simple yet sophisticated atmosphere.

The hotel's gathering places, such as the lobby, mix exquisite works of art with African handicrafts. The mixing of decorative elements in all the rooms at Saint Martin's Lane creates a unique style which defies categorization.

The double rooms and the suites have offices with onyx desks and Lucite chairs by Starck. These exclusive furnishings are combined with African stools and terra-cotta vases. Each bedroom is brightened with flowers.

Simple and practical, the 204 rooms of Saint Martin's Lane enjoy magnificent views of Covent Garden through floor-to-ceiling windows.

The bathrooms are spacious and elegant. The porcelain sink, designed by Starck, is supported by a wooden frame with a built-in shelf for towels. The large, comfortable bathtubs are free-standing; the walls are Portuguese limestone.

The recently-opened Kensington House Hotel is located in one of London's most exclusive sections, an area of feverish activity in close proximity to Kensington Palace and Gardens, major museums, famous restaurants, and the commercial districts of Knightsbridge and Earls Court. The hotel combines the tradition of the district and the building itself with a new, modern image. The four-story building, dating back to the nineteenth century, has been restored to its original elegance. The stucco details of the façade, as well as the stairs, the balustrades, and most of the plaster molding on the ceilings, were also restored. But the rooms and the Tiger bar-restaurant reflect a contemporary image defined by their simplicity and brightness. Collections of twentieth century photographs and contemporary paintings by British artists were carefully selected to complement the interior design.

Each room is different from the others in shape and size, and is provided with all the services and technology to meet the needs of business and pleasure travelers. Some have balconies, high ceilings, arches, and large windows with panoramic views of Kensington Gardens and the surrounding neighborhood. Every detail was studied to achieve an austere, modern ambience using simple lines, basic furnishings, and rich textures.

For its part, the Tiger bar-restaurant was designed as a versatile, dynamic space for morning coffee, afternoon tea, or cocktails. It also has an open area, adjacent to the entrance hall, that functions as a dining room and lounge. The blending of the classical building and the contemporary interior design creates a balanced, tranquil space.

Kensington
House Hotel

The gardens surrounding the building give the rooms a rustic atmosphere despite the hotel's location in a bustling area of the city.

The versatility of the Tiger bar-restaurant is achieved through the use of an austere interior design that combines shapes and styles of furniture in a warm ambience filled with textures and materials such as wood flooring, dark mahogany tables, and soft upholstery in vivid colors.

The décor, while achieving a modern ambience, is inspired by pieces of classical furniture and lighting that carry on a dialogue with the original character of the building.

Architects: **Charles Campbell Associates**   Interior designer: **Anne Jordan Interior Design**   Photographer: **Leonardo MediaBank**   Address: **15-16 Prince of Wales Terrace,**

London, United Kingdom Tel.: **44 207 937 2345**   Fax: **44 207 368 6700** www.hotels-london.co.uk   Opening date: **2000**   Number of rooms: **41**   Services: **restaurant, bar**

The history of the Great Eastern, the only hotel in London's financial district, speaks of the industrialization of the city, the great train stations, and the splendor of the Victorian era. The western block was finished in 1884 by Charles Barry, who also designed the Parliament building, while the eastern part, completed in 1901, was designed by Colonel W. Edis. The renovation by Manser Associates architects and interior designer Conran has revived the original Victorian spirit of the building while injecting a strong dose of modernity, which carries on a dialogue with its classical character. This becomes an aesthetic and functional challenge: to develop a shared vocabulary, modern, optimistic, singular, or comfortable, that also bears witness to the juxtaposition and complexity of these concepts.

The variety and the unique character of each space are reflected throughout the hotel. The new, imposing entrance hall, which rises in a great central cylindrical space five stories high, is comprised of basic volumes in pale colors and provides access to a striking, richly decorated private Victorian dining room.

Each of the hotel's five restaurants has its own distinctive hallmark and has direct access to the exterior, either Liverpool Street or Bishopsgate. All reclaim a piece of the building's history while carrying on a dialogue with the feverish activity characteristic of the district.

The rooms follow the same line, but are all individually decorated. With their space and light, those on the fifth and sixth floors resemble lofts, while those on the lower floors have the highest ceilings and Victorian touches. All, however, have the same modern details reflected in the colors and furnishings.

Great
Eastern Hotel

The red brickwork in the façade and the precise proportions are striking. These were highly respected and valued in the renovation work.
The building is a fine example of Victorian public architecture. For many years it was an icon among train stations.

The lobby is a clean, spare space that employs original materials, such as marble, plaster, and wood panels to create an effect with classical and modern elements.

Each restaurant tells the history of the building and its relationship to the city. The Fishmarket occupies an ornate aquamarine salon with plaster cherubs keeping watch from the friezes above. The Terminus reinterprets the classic turn-of-the-century train station buffet.

Architects: **Manser Associates**   Interior designer: **Conran & Partners**   Photographers: **Peter Cook, Jean Cazals, James Merell, Tim Winter**   Address: **Liverpool Street, London, United Kingdom**   Tel.: **44 207 618 5000** Fax: **44 207 618 5001** **www.great-eastern-hotel.co.uk**   Opening date: **February 2000**   Number of rooms: **267 (including 21 suites)**   Services: **restaurants and bars, 12 event rooms, equipment for business and conferences, shopping arcade, gym**

Previous page: The interior is also filled with classical elements that recall the era in which the hotel was built: marble stairs, plaster molding, and elegant, rich-ly-decorated meeting rooms. New uses are incorporated in a contemporary language to accommodate this aesthetic to the hotel's new requirements.

The rooms are contemporary, emphasizing comfort and functionality, while retaining classic materials and elements, such as the bathroom fixtures and floor tiles.

One Aldwych London, completed in 1907, is one of London's most emblematic Edwardian buildings. Originally the headquarters of the Morning Post, it stands at the corner of Aldwych and the Strand in Covent Garden. This district is the city's civic and financial center, is home to major theaters, fashionable shops, and art galleries, and is just a stone's throw from some of the city's most famous monuments. Its strategic location requires, of necessity, a hotel that meets the needs of business travelers as well as tourists, and it projects an image characteristic of London. Although the elegant façade seems to be intact, it has been restored, and all the decorative details and wrought-iron work at the windows have been retained.

The interior is restrained, without reference to specific time periods or styles, appropriate to both the character of the building and its location in the city. The design is more a discreet, elegant manifestation of wealth and well-being than the ostentatious luxury traditionally associated with large hotels. The premise was to minimize superfluous, excessive luxury and concentrate on the elements that really make the hotel work: service and comfort.

The key elements are rich, intense colors and textures that set the stage for a vast collection of contemporary art, which can be enjoyed in the public areas and in the rooms. The combination of decorative elements, such as the large steel mesh wall with fiber optic lights, located in the main lobby, and the Asian-style chairs designed especially for the hotel, is noteworthy.

The result is a space that can be considered both classic and modern. It has a certain solemnity, while conveying a sense of the modern and cutting-edge.

One Aldwych London

The Axis bar and restaurant is a throwback to the twenties and thirties and is a complete departure from the style of the rest of One Aldwych. The restaurant is dominated by the floor-to-ceiling mural entitled Secret City.

The surrounding space is reflected in the black lacquer of the bar. This area, like the restaurant, is two stories high. The furnishings were designed expressly for the restaurant by Fox-Linton Associates, which designed the hotel as well.

Architects: **Gordon Campbell Gray and Mary Fox-Linton**   Photographer: **Gunnar Knechtel**   Address: **One Aldwych, London, United Kingdom**   Tel. **44 20 7300 1000**   Fax: **44 20 7300 1001**   **www.onealdwych.com**   Opening date: **July 1998**   Number of rooms: **105 (includes two suites with private gyms)**   Services: **two restaurants and two bars, banquet and meeting halls, business equipment, gym**

Some of the suites have their own private gym. The rooms are decorated in variations of the same theme, but are all different. The luxurious silk drapes in solid colors contrast with the linen bed covers.

In the bathrooms, the polished brown terrazzo that covers the horizontal surfaces is striking in combination with the fixtures by Phillipe Starck and the oversize sink. The overall effect is clean and contemporary.

otting Hill is one of London's most diverse sections. Home to the traditional summer carnival and the Portobello Road market, it is also one of London's most exclusive residential districts. This diversity is apparent in the design of the Westbourne, a small hotel in the midst of this vibrant sector, which avoids the most avant-garde trends, seeking comfort in a restrained, elegant setting. The façade, in the purest Georgian style, contrasts with the interior. Here, textures and natural colors are combined in furnishings that evoke the luxury of the 1950s and are inspired by international trends. The exterior space that surrounds the hotel sets the stage for the atmosphere and the character that pervade the interior. Two Japanese gardens run from the front of the building to the rear and serve as a transition between the activity on the street and the peaceful ambience inside.

The challenge of this project was to create an alternative to the cold minimalism and luxurious excess, styles which generally mark these types of buildings, as well as to create a homey, comfortable ambience for the guest. The sensation of relaxation and tranquility is achieved through the use of the same materials, colors, and natural finishes throughout the hotel. Wood predominates and is combined with other materials, such as fabric or leather, in khaki green, bright red, or dark chocolate, and travertine in silver tones.

The bamboo work marks the transition between interior and exterior. As a complement - a feature which is truly indicative of the hotel's character - an important collection of contemporary British art adorns the public areas and the rooms.

The Westbourne Hotel

The bar and dining room are in a secluded space accessed from Westbourne Grove and from the adjoining garden. The dining area is defined by a rectangular composition reminiscent of a Mondrian work in green, mustard, and chocolate.

The ebony work on the tables and chairs harks back to the 1950s, while the combination of decorative elements creates a sense of informality.

Architect: **Giles Baker**   Photographer: **Gunnar Knechtel**   Address: **163-165 Westbourne Grove, London, United Kingdom**   Tel.: **44 207 243 6008**   Fax: 44 207 229 7204

Opening date: **September 2000**   Number of rooms: **20**   Services: **bar, restaurant, business equipment, DVD, laundry**

Each room has a different style of bed and a variety
of finishes for the walls, ceilings, drapes, and floating shelves.
The woods used include tropical olive, Indian laurel,
Japanese ash, and American walnut.

n the heart of the Irish capital, surrounded by Georgian architecture, is the Morrison Dublin Hotel, which offers a diversity of special qualities in the most contemporary design. Although the size and exterior of the building are in keeping with the scale and rhythm of the surrounding district, the interior is a catalog of outstanding spaces resulting from the experimentation with new materials and finishes. The internal organization makes it possible to merge two areas with completely different sets of features. On the one hand, there are the public areas, such as the lobby and boisterous bars. On the other hand, there are the much quieter rooms, linked by a wall that runs the length of the building. The wall separates the rooms while also linking them vertically and horizontally. With this geometry the spaces flow tranquilly into each other. There is direct access from the lobby to the two-story restaurant, the stairs to the café, or the bar - without even passing through a door.

High-ceilinged spaces were created despite the extra effort this entailed in terms of achieving adequate climate control. Lighting is rarely direct: it is almost always hidden behind screens or built into the walls. The result is a soft, warm ambience. Although geometric lines and simple shapes predominate, the space is enhanced by a carefully thought-out range of colors and textures incorporated into the furnishings and décor. The rooms, designed along the same lines, include an array of decorative touches from fine white linen to soft leather, dark woods or heavy carpets of thick wool. The end result is a space of balanced dialogue between apparent disorder and a comfortable, tranquil setting.

Morrison
Hotel Dublin

A north-south axis runs the entire length of the building. This is reflected in the longitudinal layout of the lobby and the upper-floor hallways, and is used to create interesting visual touches.

The proportions of the dining room, which can be viewed from the public areas of the building, make this a dynamic space, often frequented by customers who are not hotel guests.

Architect: **Douglas Wallace**   Designer: **John Rocha**   Photographer: **Andrew Bradley**   Address: **1 Ormond Quay, Dublin, Ireland**   Tel.: **353 1 887 2400**   Fax: **353 1 878 3185**

www.morrisonhotel.ie   Number of rooms: **94**   Services: **voice messaging, ISDN lines, mini-bar, restaurant, bar, health center, meeting rooms**

The predominant colors in the public areas are carefully limited to browns, blacks, creams, and grays, with touches of red. But the materials are rich and diverse. The floors are limestone and stained oak, the walls are polished plaster and oak panels, the drapes are silk and velvet, and the carpets are handmade.

The furnishings, made especially for the hotel, complement the modern character and richness of the materials. They range from loveseats to leather armchairs to white canvas chairs for dining.

A collection of more than 120 contemporary paintings, reserved exclusively for the hotel, adorns all the public areas and the rooms.

eeting the requirements of a luxury hotel in such a limited space while making the interior look and feel comfortable was this project's major architectural challenge. The Hotel Square, located in one of the most exclusive parts of Paris, sits on a small triangular lot, just 535 square feet. The hotel is built around a 30 feet high half-cylinder which accommodates the staircases and from which the rest of the spaces branch off. This staircase is topped by a spherical glass skylight that has become a symbol of the structure. Behind the Indian green granite façade of this austere building, located in one of the most exclusive parts of Paris, there is a sophisticated atmosphere, an ambience without reference to any era or style, in which the predominant element is comfort.

The interior was designed so that every niche has its own character. Each of the 18 rooms and 4 suites is unique, and the decorative touches, while using a common language, are in keeping with the special qualities of each space. The lobby, the stairway, and the reading room were conceived as a gallery for displaying contemporary art. In contrast to the bright materials, smooth surfaces, and cold atmosphere of the public areas, the rooms have a warmer, secluded feel, thanks to the decorative elements. In the rooms, natural materials and fibers in ivory and gray, brick and saffron, or bronze and gold predominate, while all the bathrooms are done in Carrara marble. Luxury, nearly always associated with huge spaces on a grand scale, is achieved here with a well-conceived layout and special attention to the details and finishings.

Hotel
Square

The building is hermetic, with basic lines, and covered with a continuous skin of granite and glass.

The entrance, in the middle of the building's side, is as discreet as the rest of the structure.

The traditional reception desk was replaced with a warm piece in keeping with the building's proportions to create a more personal setting.

Architect: F. X. Evellin   Designer: Patrick Derderian   Photographer: Pere Planells   Address: 3 Rue de Boulainvilliers, Paris, France   Tel.: 33 1 44 14 91 90   Fax: 33 1 44 14 91 99   www.hotelsquare.com   Opening date: 1997   Number of rooms: 22   Services: restaurant, bar, fax, voice messaging, air-conditioning, mini-bar, cable TV, room service, laundry

The stairway is enhanced by the formal play of curved and straight lines between different levels. It becomes a source of natural light as well as a meeting place.

The Zebra Restaurant, on the ground floor, has the spatial features of a loft. It is an unbroken space containing decorative touches and comfortable furniture, accommodating 160 people.

Although the hotel is small, the rooms and suites are remarkable for their spaciousness. Each has a different layout and a set of colors reflected in the decorative elements, natural fabrics, and finishes.

Carrara marble covers the entire bathroom. The combination of marble, chrome fixtures, and mirrors affords a sense of spaciousness and brightness.

Arrondissement number 7, Paris, where the hotel Montalembert is located, is one of the city's most exclusive and elegant. In an upper-class residential section, it enjoys a tranquil atmosphere despite its strategic location in the heart of the city, in close proximity to Paris icons including the Eiffel Tower, the Champ de Mars, the Musée d'Orsay, and the Louvre.

After a year of remodeling, the hotel has reopened its doors to reveal a renewed style that values its original character. Carefully finished, using a contemporary language, it retains the building's spirit. Elements of the façade, interior details, and decorative touches were saved. The existing blue and white color palette was expanded to a range that reinforces the idea of a dialogue between classical and contemporary elements.

The feeling of spaciousness in the main lobby was achieved through the use of fine materials original to the building, and a careful selection of furniture, decorative elements, and lighting. The carpet which once covered the entrance and stairs – displaying the hotel's logo – was removed to reveal natural marble tiles. This space, enriched by a classic 1920s staircase, serves as a backdrop for a combination of furniture styles that share the same formal language. Low sofas, chairs, and couches upholstered in white leather or gray or dark iron-colored velvet are combined to create a warm, comfortable ambience. The piece de resistance of this minimalist approach to furnishings was provided by the carefully-placed slender lamps of iron and bronze.

Hotel Montalembert

The inclusion of classic decorative objects and antiques reinforces the notion of restoring the hotel's original character without sacrificing the comfort provided by modern sofas and novel textures.

All the rooms offer different design solutions while employing warm tones, wood, and linen. The lighting sets off the construction details and the photographs and etchings by Giuseppe Castiglioni, which add the finishing touch to the décor.

The terrace at the rear recalls the nineteenth century private garden and serves as an extension of the restaurant.

Designer: **Grace Leo-Andrieu**   Photographer: **Gilles Trillard**   Address: **3, rue de Montalembert, Paris, France**   Tel.: **33 1 45 49 68 68**   Fax: **33 1 45 49 69 49**

www.montalembert.com   Opening date: **2001**   Number of rooms: **56**   Services: **bar, restaurant, conference room**

The image of this luxury hotel responds to the needs of Maastricht, a small city in the south of Holland that is welcoming a growing number of tourists. Despite its history as a Roman city with a vast, well-preserved architectural legacy, its popularity is based largely on its cultural activity and its strategic location, right on the border with Belgium and Germany. The project gave this nineteenth century building, so characteristic of the city, a fresh face by incorporating elements of color and light into the façade. Entry is through a long corridor, decorated in intense tones, which leads to the main lobby. Looking at it from the street is like looking into a shop window.

Tranquility, comfort, and contrast sum up the character of the hotel's interior. The designers chose to use a minimum amount of furnishings, with a restrained language, where points of color provide warmth. The sofas in the lobby, the chairs in the lounge, and the stools in the bar are upholstered in dark leather and blend with the similarly-colored bookshelves and woodwork. While the lounges are done in browns, blacks, and grays to blend with the wood and achieve a warm, peaceful atmosphere, the traffic areas use lighter, more cheerful colors for a sensation of freshness and dynamism.

The rooms employ the same concepts: minimal furnishings, same color palette, and points of color that recreate the ambience of the public areas.

La Bergère

The decorative elements of the façade were preserved and restored, as were the wrought-iron
detailing of the balconies and windows. At street
level, the look was completely changed. The
transparency achieved through the use of large
windows allows for more complete integration of
the exterior with the interior.

The traffic areas contain some elements of color, which are striking in a space where white predominates. Light enters the lobby from a courtyard that runs the length of the building.

Architect: **Maarten Engelman**   Interior design: **Feran Thomassen**   Photographer: **Pere Planells**   Address: **Stationsstraat 40 Maastricht, Holland**   Tel.: **31 43 3282526**

Fax: **31 43 3282526**   **www.la-bergere.com**   Number of rooms: **76**   Services: **library, gym, shops, bar, restaurant**

In the rooms, large photographs above the headboards dominate the area. Flexible, built-in furnishings make the most efficient use of space.

Previous page: A light sliding door can be opened to integrate the bathroom into the main part of the room, enhancing the perception of spaciousness.

The details of the furnishings and accessories complement the décor as points of color that add a sense of cheer.

The Widder sits in the middle of a quiet Zurich neighborhood. It's a cozy hotel that retains the characteristic style of eight original houses of the historic downtown area while including contemporary elements. The buildings that comprise the hotel are the only surviving part - now a national monument - of an Augustinian monastery built in the thirteenth century. They were carefully restored between 1990 and 1995, including new technologies to equip the building for its new use. The 42 rooms, 7 suites, meeting rooms, and banquet halls were integrated into the ancient buildings with great sensitivity and an innovative architectural approach.

The conversion plan does more than meet all the needs of a five-star hotel. It also provides something that is becoming less and less common in these types of projects: privacy in every sense of the word. To start with, and in keeping with the character of the original buildings, no two rooms are alike, and some have a private balcony. Every room is unique in terms of its floor plan, furnishings, layout, and style. So the atmosphere is closer to that of a highly-refined private residence in which each space has its own language.

This takes into account the need to accommodate other types of activities. Six different rooms for banquets and meetings, each retaining their original character and each clearly different from the others, are equipped with the latest technology needed for these events. The new materials used for the project, such as metal, glass, and painted wood or leather panels, contrast with and stand out from the textures of the brick or rustic wood of the original buildings. The result is a warm, cozy ambience with all the modern applications required for maximum comfort.

Widder
Hotel

The character of the original buildings was respected inside and out. The floors, the rustic wood paneling on the walls, and the ceiling structure are original details.

The skylight that replaced the roof in one of the buildings converted this space, now used as a restaurant, into an area which is flooded with light but isolated from the immediate neighbors.

Architect: **Tilla Theus**   Photographer: **Miquel Tres**   Address: **Rennweg 7, Zurich, Switzerland**   Tel.: **41 1 224 2526**   Fax: **41 1 224 2424**   **www.widderhotel.ch**

Opening date: **March 1995**   Number of rooms: **49 (including 7 suites)**   Services: **6 rooms for events and conferences, restaurant, bar**

The contemporary language with which the new materials are used respects to a large extent, the original structure.

The furniture that was chosen for the public areas and the rooms is comprised of comfortable and austere elements which, far from trying to dominate the space, complement it.

The intimate and private ambience that was sought in every corner of the project is emphasized by the lighting. A play of chiaroscuro and indirect lighting brings out certain niches and hides others in the same space.

n downtown Zurich, minutes from the city's major attractions, this 19-room hotel captures, in its interior design, the area's metropolitan spirit. The combination of intense cultural and financial activity and the historical legacy of restrained architecture make downtown Zurich a vibrant setting, rich in small urban anecdotes.

The first thing that stands out about the Seehof is its transparency vis-à-vis the exterior. Outdoor activities merge with the interior, not just aesthetically, but functionally as well. So the hotel becomes another slice of the urban route, as important to tourists as it is to local residents. The entrance area is one large piece of glass, like a shop window, through which the entire interior is visible. It is accessed through the box-shaped, metal-framed main door.

In sharp contrast to the cold, austere façade, the interior is a warm space decorated with wood and earth tones. The basic furniture is inspired by simple geometric lines, reflected in the interior renovation work. The lines and cubic shapes are evident in the bar, the wall niches, and the lights, which were designed especially for the hotel and are shaped like wooden boxes suspended from the ceiling. This language continues into the rooms, which are done in softer tones – from white to pearl gray – and achieve a sense of tranquility, eschewing any decorative excess.

Hotel
Seehof

The Seehof bar is open to the public as well as
hotel guests. Its urban character is accented by
basic, informal furnishings

Architects: **Frei & Ehrensperger**   Photographer: **Miquel Tres**   Address: **Seehofstrasse 11, Zurich, Switzerland**   Tel.: **41 1 254 5757**   Fax: **41 1 254 5758**
www.hotelseehof.ch Opening date: **April 1999** Number of rooms: **19** Services: **restaurant, bar, fax, data port**

The restaurant is open until midnight. Chef
Keisuke Takatori prepares a selection of fresh
seasonal dishes every day.

he Diplomatic, part of the AC Hotel chain, is located in one of the most emblematic sections of Barcelona, the Ensanche. This extensive area, developed in the mid nineteenth century, boasts some of the finest examples of modern Catalonian architecture. It is also the city's most congested district, known for a wide range of activities, making it a magnet for visitors. The hotel is a stone's throw from the paseo de Grà-cia, avenida Diagonal, and plaza Catalunya, in the heart of the commercial, cultural, and financial district.

The existing building was rehabilitated to serve multiple functions while providing a restrained, tranquil setting that meets every guest's needs. The basic objective was to provide the building with all the necessities, in terms of contemporary design and new technologies, to achieve the high level of comfort and the formal language common to and representative of the AC hotel chain.

The staircase, with stainless steel and glass handrails, dominates a two-story space which houses the public areas. The main lobby and reception area are organized around a central rectangular space dominated by polished natural stone walls. The space is broken by columns and dividing panels finished with wood or mirrors, and the small spaces created by these dividers contain furnishings that use the same formal language as the rest of the interior. Basic geometrical lines, dark wood, cotton cushions, natural fiber carpeting, and dimmer lighting define these areas.

This language is the basis of a sequence of planned visual effects. The same materials, textures, and colors are used throughout the reception area, lounges, library, and rooms.

Hotel
Diplomatic

The project was conceived around the building's original stylistic elements. The façade and access areas have a timeless international image.

The two-story space housing the stairway uses natural stone, stainless steel, and glass to create a light, bright setting.

While the traffic areas are defined by cold tones achieved through the use of elements such as mirrors and gray colors, the lounges, with wood panels, more comfortable furnishings, and soft lighting, have a warmer atmosphere.

Architects: GCA Arquitectos   Photographer: Jordi Miralles   Address: Pau Claris, 122, Barcelona, España   Tel. 34 932 723 810   Fax 34 932 723 811   www.ac-hoteles.com

Number of rooms: 211   Services: restaurant, bar, business equipment, air conditioning, mini-bar, parking, 24 hour room service, data ports

Dark wood display cases divide the different areas of the bar and provide indirect lighting.

Basic geometric shapes, squares and lines, are employed throughout the interior space and the decorative details, unifying the materials and textures.

HOTEL DIPLOMATIC

ASIA

Akasaka Prince

Devi Gahr

Akasaka is one of Tokyo's most vibrant, dynamic districts. Just minutes from the city's civic and commercial centers, it is a hot spot of cultural activity and nightlife. The modern, 40-floor building that houses this hotel, designed by architect Kenzo Tange and part of the Prince chain, stands as a symbol of the district and contrasts with the small scale and tranquil atmosphere of the surrounding area. The building's staggered vertical sections form a concave space, making the powerful structure seem lighter while achieving more façade surface area, thus providing abundant natural light and affording views of the city. The exterior, finished with materials such as steel and glass, strengthens the building's image as an international hotel with all the characteristic features of space, technology, and comfort.

Inside, the spaces are ample and are accentuated by the use of materials, color, and light. Brightness is achieved through reflections from mirrors, glass, and marble. Repetition of basic pieces of furniture in the public spaces provides a decorative texture that accents their size and neutral character. The rooms have an average area of 460 square feet and all have a large corner window affording impressive views and abundant light. The décor makes extensive use of shiny textures and colors such as white, pearl gray, and silver.

Akasaka Prince

The various public areas, meeting rooms, and small restaurants have very different atmospheres. The cocktail lounge on the fortieth floor affords magnificent views of the city from an intimate space, while the design of the mirrors and the interior of the Crystal Palace banquet hall create a magical space accommodating up to 1600 guests.

The Kioi restaurant offers a seasonal menu featuring fresh ingredients in a typical Japanese ambience.

Architect: **Kenzo Tange**   Photographer: **Akasaka Prince files**   Address: **1-2 Kio-cho, Chiyoda-ku, Tokyo, Japan**   Tel.: **03 3234 1111**   Fax: **03 3262 5163**

www.princehotels.co.jp   Opening date: **1990**   Number of rooms: **761**   Services: **13 restaurants and bars, business center**

The Japanese suites are divided into two peaceful areas decorated with traditional furnishings which contrast with the impressive views.

All the rooms are generous in size and have large beds.

The homey suites have spaces, such as living rooms
or studios, that are separate from the bedrooms.

The walled palace, Devi Garh, protected by a small valley in the Aravali Mountains, was built in the eighteenth century as a defensive fort and is one of the three major passes along the Udaipur Valley, state of Rajasthan, in northwestern India. The original building was erected around 1760 by order of Raghudev Singh II, but due to its strategic location and the constant wars against Mughal invaders, it was subsequently altered. It was finally abandoned in the 1960s after the principality merged with the state of Rajasthan. The complex, imposing building, 13 miles from the nearest city, is surrounded by a natural landscape of rugged mountains, narrow plains, and sparse vegetation stretching out through the valleys.

After years of restoration and reconstruction, the building has been fitted out with the goal of reopening its doors, this time as a luxury hotel. Each of its 23 suites is individually decorated in a floral, landscape, or chromatic scheme that makes it unique, with a character all its own. The hotel also boasts seven tents that recreate the habitat of the rajputs, ancient and renowned expeditionaries of the region.

The project was conceived as a meeting place of the traditional past and modern India in which the interior design and the decorative details are especially noteworthy. This was achieved through the use of traditional materials such as local marble, semi-precious stones, wood, bamboo mats, and natural canvas in a restrained, minimalist language. The simple geometric lines of the new elements are striking, and engage in dialogue with the stone carvings, textures, and complex shapes of the existing structure. The contemporary design and this spectacular legacy are complemented with high-tech services that meet the needs of today's guests.

Devi Gahr

The furnishings in the common areas were inspired by traditional lines and pieces reinterpreted in an austere, monochromatic language.

The main swimming pool, located in the old palace gardens, enjoys an intimate atmosphere while taking advantage of a panoramic view of the Udaipur Valley.

Architects: **Gautam Bhatia and Naveen Gupta**   Interior designer: **Rajiv Saini**   Photographer: **Amit Pasricha**   Address: **Village Delwara, Rajasthan, India**
Tel.: **91 2953 89211**   Fax: **91 2953 89357**   **www.deviresorts.com**   Opening date: **1997**   Number of rooms: **23 (all suites)**   Services: **restaurant, banquet halls, business equipment, gym, spa, beauty salon, library, 24-hour room service.**

Each of the suites, inspired by the landscape or the palace itself, acquires an identity all its own through the use of materials or a predominant color.

Most of the furniture is made from the same materials: stone, marble, or wood. These are complemented by mats, cushions, and special decorative furnishings and pieces.

AUSTRALIA

Kirketon

On a narrow street across from the Kings Cross fire station, this hotel is perfectly situated for those who want a unique taste of Sydney. Darlinghurst is one of the oldest and most interesting suburbs, on top of a hill and equidistant from the most emblematic districts and downtown. A century ago it was filled with the mansions of the upper-middle class and the new colonists, many of which still remain. But this area is even more famous for its café society, bohemian culture, and eclectic mix of the old and new. This diversity creates a vibrant atmosphere reminiscent of New York's Soho district.

The relationship that existed between the client and the designer from the very beginning was vital to the project's success. The client wanted to create a boutique-style setting and functionalism, so the design conveys a subtle urbanism marked by the characteristics of the area that surrounds it. The project respects the original scale of the building, which dates from the 1920s, while reflecting an appropriate austerity in elements such as the materials, the details, and the atmosphere. A whimsical mix of classic twentieth century, contemporary, and antique furnishings can be found in every corner. The real challenge was to separate the different spaces and functions while using the same formal language throughout. A rational approach to design and modest use of the materials form the backdrop to a fine layer of contemporary style.

The Kirketon Hotel is clearly part of a new architectural movement that is sweeping away old trends no longer considered desirable in Sydney. The project, which embodies a strict approach to an architectural renovation project, is a minimalist, refined alternative to the impersonal international style.

Kirketon

The project incorporates details by prestigious Australian designers. The signs are by the Fabio Ongarato team, the uniforms are by Peter Morrissey, the bathrooms are by Aesop, and the kitchen is the domain of Luke Mangan, chef of the hotel's main restaurants.

A uniform color scheme and dearth of decorative elements create a peaceful, sophisticated setting for the entrance and reception area.

Every space is comprised of basic geometric shapes and elements. This is evident in the flooring and in each and every detail.

Architects: **Burley Katon Halliday Architects**   Photographer: **Sharin Rees**   Address: **229 Darlinghurst Rd., Sydney, Australia**   Tel.: **61 2 9332 2011** Fax: **61 2 9332 2499**

www.kirketon.com.au   Opening date: **1999**   Number of rooms: **40**   Services: **restaurant, bar, business facilities, secretarial service, air conditioning, mini-bar, parking**

The design gave special importance to every corner of the project. The restrooms, at the end of a corridor, add an element of surprise to the lobby - a set of mirrors and transparent surfaces that create a scenographic effect.

The entire first floor encompasses lifestyle elements that emphasize the importance of careful design and fine service.

The hotel's restaurants and bars are internationally famous. Salt, the finest restaurant, and its chef, Luke Mangan, have received independent awards, earning recognition as the culinary phenomenon of Sydney.

All the rooms - 16 junior, 16 premium, and 8 executive - pay careful attention to aesthetic and functional details to ensure that the clients' needs are satisfied. All have working windows, mirrored headboards, smooth surfaces, and interesting textures, including angora and linen fabrics, soft leather, and wood. They also have communication and audio systems, data ports, air conditioning, and full room service.

The various pieces of furniture and the lighting produce a play of colors that personalizes each room and creates a distinctive atmosphere.

AMERICA

The Hotel Miami

Whitelaw

Delano

The Marcel

The Bentley

Dylan Hotel

Although the idea of the hotel-boutique has become popular in the last two decades, when the Sunset Marquis first opened its doors in the sixties, it was a completely innovative concept. It is an exclusive, cozy hotel whose 108 rooms are suites carefully designed to make the guest feel at home. Adjacent to the main building are twelve small villas with private patios, reminiscent of the south of France. To ensure that the hotel met the latest aesthetic and functional requirements, the building was renovated by designers Olivia Villaluz and Barry Salehian and reopened in 1999. The project drastically changed the image of the entire hotel, wrapping it in calmness and serenity.

The renovation incorporated a new aesthetic language, visible in the lobby and dining room. The new materials that enrich the space, such as slate, marble, mohair, and Murano glass, shape an ambience of relaxing textures accented by a soft palette of greens, yellows, and deep grays. The high ceilings and opulent glass doors create a fresh space flooded with light, while solid, well-proportioned furnishings give it a human scale. The rooms are sanctuaries in which the guests are surrounded by similar materials and colors.

The sofas, chairs, tables, and shelves were designed by the interior decorators themselves, avoiding any allusion to the latest fashions or to a broad range of historical references. A variety of lamps with a suggestion of curves illuminate the space while accenting the rigidity of the other furnishings' straight lines. Each suite is designed, in form and function, to accommodate a variety of activities from the most intimate dinner to a casual cocktail.

Sunset
Marquis

From the outside, the proportions of the hotel suggest a domesticity which is accented by the use of the materials. The jade green slate in the lobby is played off against the wood panels in the reception area, which are arranged in a similar pattern.

The furniture is designed around basic lines and shapes and is camouflaged by its monochromatic character, fading into the background, avoiding the trendy and avant-garde.

Architects: **Olivia Villaluz and Barry Salehian**   Photographer: **Undine Pröhl**   Address: **1200 North Alta Loma Road, West Hollywood, United States**   Tel.: **310 657 1333**   Fax: **310 652 5300**   **www.sunsetmarquishotel.com**   Original opening date: **1963**   Opening date after renovation: **1999**   Number of rooms: **108 suites and 12 villas**   Services: **restaurant, bar, spa, gym**

The common areas achieve intimacy through the proportions of the furnishings, the use of drapes, and the austere décor.

Earth tones in combination with pale yellows and greens were chosen to achieve a warm ambience in the rooms without resorting to decorative excesses.

California is the perfect setting for this small hotel, which recreates the aesthetics and the atmosphere of mid-twentieth century America. In the 1950s, as the end result of industrialization and rampant consumerism, various icons of modern American and European design - Neutra, Raymond, and Loewy, among others – created a new and different appearance for practically everything, from buildings and furniture to cars and can openers. The American dream of technology linked to comfort and an individual, novel aesthetic becomes reality through the design of each element. The project attempted not only to solve problems of form and function, but to create an entire lifestyle and, above all, to enjoy it.

The Orbit In has 10 rooms with furniture and décor by famous American designers of the 40s, 50s, and 60s in a setting typical of the United States' west coast. The San Jacinto Mountains shelter the building, surrounding it with spectacular views of the region's rough, desert valleys.

Located in Palm Springs' historic Tennis Club District, the hotel recalls a time when aperitifs at poolside and lounge music were the popular ways to relax. Each space was planned and restored to reflect the design concepts the architects and designers brought to the desert in the 50s, perhaps seeking a setting in which they could bring their cutting-edge ideas to life. The classic American kitchens and the pink-tiled bathrooms are restorations of those that originally existed in the building. Furniture by Eames, Saarinen, Bertoia, Nelson, Noguchi, and Schultz, combined with contemporary design and photography, make the hotel a true and memorable oasis.

Orbit In

Each detail, like an image frozen in time and protected by the imposing valley that surrounds it, refers to the American model in which modernity was linked to an aesthetic of basic lines, rational compositions, and functionality.

Architects: **Herbert W. Burns + Lance O'Donell**   Photographer: **Undine Pröhl**   Address: **562 W. Arenas, Palm Springs, United States**   Tel.: **760 323 3585**   Fax: **760 323 3599**

www.orbitin.com   Opening date: **February 2000**   Number of rooms: **10**   Services: **restaurant, bar, gym, swimming pool, 24-hour room service**

The Hotel, now one of the most luxurious and exotic hotels in Miami Beach, was once a modest hotel known as the Tiffany. Built in 1939 by architect L. Murray Dixon, it retains all its art deco details. After a complete renovation, it has reopened its doors with a mix of the building's original character and a sophisticated image achieved through very careful interior design.

The main challenge was to reconcile the sense of functionality with a fantastic, eccentric place. The sun, sea, and sky are the basis for the design and decorative themes and the attractive color palette. A wide range of blues and whites illuminate the façade, while warm tones create a unique sensation of vitality and peace inside. The furniture was inspired by the original geometry of the building, the shapes, the designs in the flooring, and the openings in the façade. The upholstery, which combines colors such as mustard, parrot green, and lilac, adds a tropical touch. The rooms use the same color schemes, adding grays for a heightened sense of tranquility.

A spectacular view can be enjoyed from the top-floor terrace, where the pool is located. A wooden deck serves as a backdrop for the different shades of blue of the sky, sea, and pool. The resplendent white furniture and massage booths recall a Caribbean island or perhaps a place lost in the desert.

This hotel's balance is achieved through the element of surprise and the combination of the building's original style with a contemporary renovation using very attractive shapes, textures, and colors.

The Hotel Miami

The Wish, a restaurant under the direction of Andrea Curto, is decorated in the art deco style. A palette of fresh colors and furniture with restrained lines create a cozy atmosphere in which to enjoy the delicious dishes prepared by its renowned chef.

Interior designer: **Todd Oldham**   Photographer: **Pep Escoda**   Address: **801 Collins Avenue, Miami Beach, United States**   Tel.: **305 531 2222**   Fax: **305 531 3222**

www.thehotelofsouthbeach.com   Opening date: **1998**   Number of rooms: **52 (incluides 4 suites)**   Services: **restaurant, banquet halls, beauty shop, business equipment, gym, swimming pool, parking**

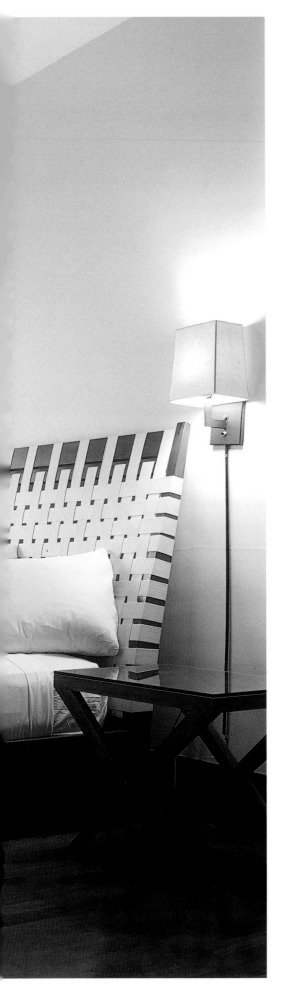

What makes this small South Beach hotel special is that the renovation - which combines the building's art deco features with contemporary art and design - includes touches in keeping with its tropical surroundings. So it is more reflective of the Latino side of Miami while providing a niche that is removed from the tourist frenzy. The building, one more jewel of the city's art deco district, was built in 1939 by architect Henry Hohauser on the southern part of Ocean Drive, one of the district's most popular streets. After completion of the changes designed by Brian Stoner, which won several awards, including Miami's Design Art Deco Preservation Award, it has opened its doors with a renewed image, but without abandoning its original character.

The mix of styles incorporates different textures, materials, and furnishings. The main lobby boasts furniture by designer Ron Arad and works by artist Willie Moser, all specially created for the hotel. Pieces from the 1950s and 1960s set the tone in the lounges, while the restaurant and rooms have a more tropical theme. In the rooms, pale earth or sand tones mix with loungers, chairs, and headboards covered with natural color canvas strips. In the restaurant, the dark wood flooring stands out against the chairs with lighter-colored wooden slats, the natural canvas drapes, and the backdrop of palm trees.

The tasteful understatement with which the building was remodeled and the decorative elements that were combined speaks to the hotel's historic position as a counterpoint to an increasingly exhibitionist setting.

The
Century
Hotel

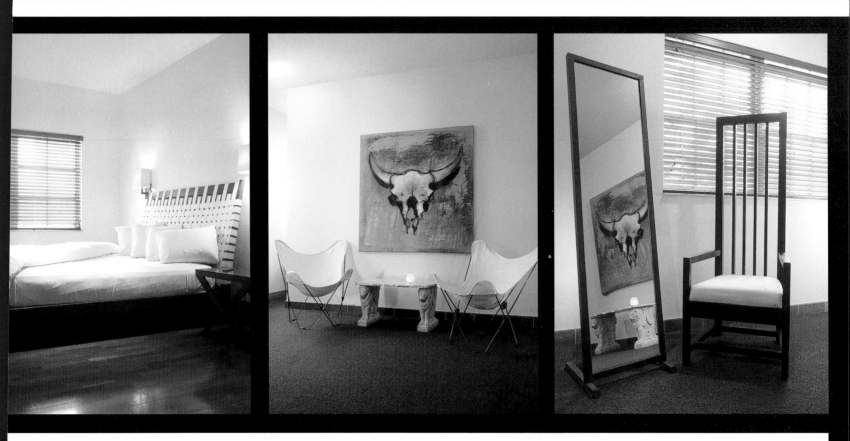

While the building's exterior retains its iconic character as if stuck in time, the interior includes the latest technologies for service and comfort.

The room furnishings, colors, and decorations are in similar tones and use the minimum number of elements to create a harmonious, tranquil setting.

Architect: **Brian Stoner**   Photographer: **Pep Escoda**   Address: **140 Ocean Drive, Miami Beach, United States**   Tel.: **305 674 8855**   Fax: **305 538 5733**

www.centuryhotelsobe.com   Opening date: **October 2000**   Number of rooms: **31**   Services: **restaurant, bar, gym, spa.**

tarting out as a classical structure with infinite possibilities for modern interpretation, the Royal Hotel became a fusion of eras, styles, and shapes. The building dates to 1938 and is part of the art deco architectural legacy of Miami's South Beach district. After falling on hard times, it is now reopening its doors, having been transformed into a suggestive mix of past, present, and future. The new Royal, now part of the Raven chain, merges the character of the 1930s with the latest trends in design and technology to create an ambience in which the visitor feels as though he has traveled back in time. Structural elements, details of the façade and the sign, were restored and merged with contemporary design elements, especially furnishings. The project is in tune with one of the most dynamic and active revitalized areas of Miami. The hotel is located in the midst of the commercial and tourist district, two blocks from the beach and very close to downtown.

Every one of the 42 rooms combines classic materials, such as the marble flooring, with pieces of furniture designed by the architect especially for the hotel, such as the modular floating headboard that also functions as a bar. The palette of colors chosen for the interior spaces is striking, combining purple tones with pale green, orange, and blue - a departure from the style of the building reminiscent of the pop art of the sixties and seventies.

Despite the aesthetic considerations, the main objective of the design was to create a comfortable, salutary setting, rather than a particular style. This small hotel includes two suites, a restaurant, a bar, and a second-floor terrace from which to enjoy a panoramic view of South Beach.

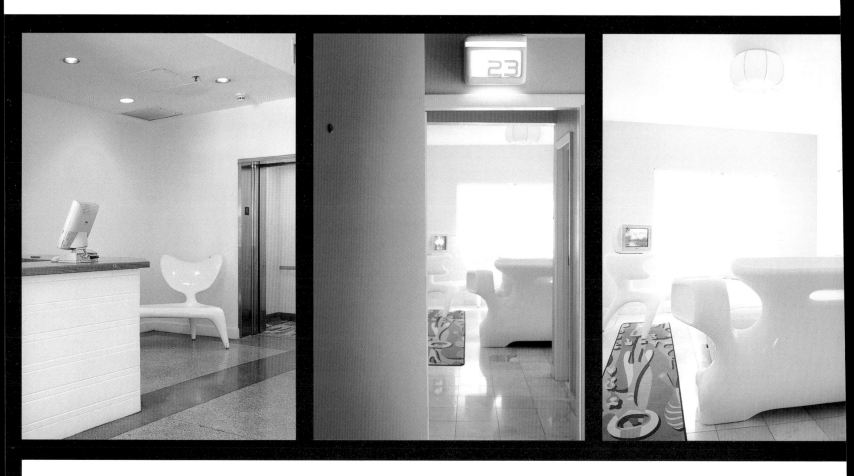

The contemporary elements mingle with the
existing elements and the building's proportions
to create a cheerful, carefree setting.

The carpets, designed by the architect himself,
burst like a suggestive color image into spaces
dominated by pale tones.

The furniture, specially designed for the hotel, is made of a plastic resin that accentuates the brightness and light of the space.

Architect: **Jordan Mozer**   Photographer: **Pep Escoda**   Address: **758 Washington Avenue, Miami Beach, United States**   Tel.: **305 673 9009**   Fax: **305 673 9244**

www.royalhotelsouthbeach.com   Opening date: **2000**   Number of rooms: **42**   Services: **restaurant, bar, business equipment, 24 hour room service**

ocated at 808 Collins Avenue, just steps from the beach, the Whitelaw Hotel is an affordable alternative in the popular and very busy area of Miami Beach. In contrast to the big chain hotels and the excessive luxury of many local hotels, the Whitelaw is summed up by its advertising slogan: "Clean sheets, hot water, and stiff drinks." This premise is reflected in the interior design of the building, which was renovated using a contemporary language that makes reference to the style of the 1970s while rescuing and valuing its own history.

Originally designed as a hotel, it was used as a training base during World War II. In its heyday it was considered the most modern hotel on the beach, perhaps in part because it was the first to have an elevator. The renovation respected all the structural elements and preserved the art deco details that characterize the architecture of that era.

Without resorting to grandiose designs, the project pays special attention to the roof and original windows with their simple and concentric geometric lines. This is reflected in the interior by both the use of period pieces and new contemporary objects in the same style.

The lobby is filled with natural light and feels airy and spacious. It makes extensive use of clear and translucent glass, mirrors, and the color white, not just in the architecture, but also in the furnishings and decorative touches. The result is an alternative – in design and budget – in the very popular South Beach section.

Whitelaw

The façade retains the original details of the 1936 building and inspired the interior decor.

The play of transparencies among the different areas of the lobby and between the interior and exterior areas makes this small space seem larger.

The ceramic flooring, the details of the doorway arches, and the ceiling molding are part of the building's original design and set the stage for the decorative objects and lighting by Artemide and Flos.

Architect: **Alan Liberman**   Photographer: **Pep Escoda**   Address: **808 Collins Avenue, Miami Beach, United States**   Tel.: **305 398 7000**   Fax: **305 398 7010**

www.whitehotel.com   Opening date: **January 2000**   Number of rooms: **49**   Services: **bar, restaurant, business equipment, laundry service**

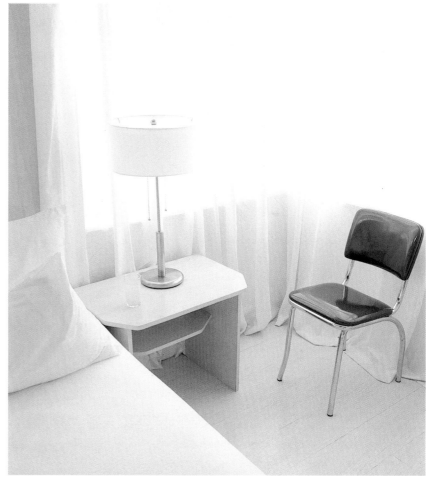

From the moment it opened, the Delano, in Miami Beach, started a new hotel trend: the urban resort. Located in the heart of one of the most visited and vital cities in the United States, it affords the balance of a space of total calm and relaxation in the midst of explosive urban activity, night life, and exuberant energy. It is a project that harmoniously synthesizes the vitality of the sector, respecting the symbolic and historic character of the building by creating tranquil, peaceful settings.

The project's aim was to pay homage to the spirit of the American family while offering a pure, elegant response to an era characterized by the excess of design. The main lobby, conceived as a space with an ambiguous relationship between interior and exterior, is a refined place where the ideas of hotel as theater and as a socializing space come together. As nightclubs were the place to meet in the seventies and restaurants were in the eighties, the hotel lobby has been, since the nineties, the center of social activity and has sparked special interest in how these types of spaces are configured. The plan for the Delano takes this concept as a point of departure for the development of the design. The entrance is comprised of nine spaces, each conceived as functionally and formally independent and which, taken as a whole, afford the sensation of a small village woven together out of different characteristics. A complete overhaul of the lobby area, doing away with any conventional distinction, creates an ambiguous separation between interior and exterior. The furnishings, lighting, and interior décor emphasize this contrast through a series of pieces that combine the building's classical style with the most contemporary design. The result is an ambivalent space where the visitor can find himself in the center of activity or in an oasis of calm and relaxation.

Delano

The hotel lobby is a gallery of furniture design. It contains an international collection of more than 650 pieces by famous twentieth century designers, including Antoni Gaudí, Man Ray, Charles and Ray Eames, Salvador Dalí, Mark Newson, and Philippe Starck, who designed the hotel.

Designer: **Philippe Starck**   Photographer: **Pep Escoda**   Address: **1685 Collins Avenue, Miami Beach, United States**   Tel.: **305 672 2000**   Fax: **305 532 0099**

Opening date: **June 1995**   Number of rooms: **208**   Services: **restaurant for banquets, business equipment, gym, 24 hour room service, private pools**

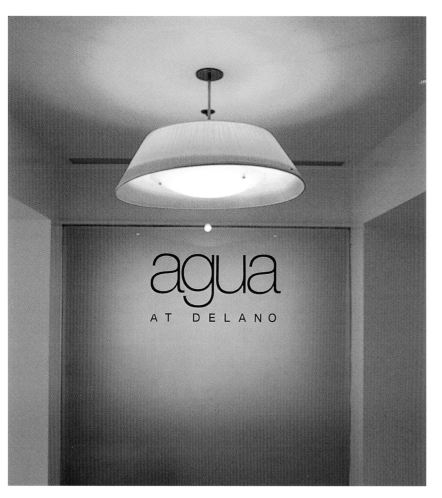

The rooms were restored to create a luxurious and comfortable setting. White and pearl gray tones predominate, not just on the walls and floors, but in all the furnishings and decorative touches. A layer of cork was installed under the floor to enhance soundproofing, while the wooden flooring sports a fine, shiny finish.

Most of the rooms have a private exterior area as intimate as the rooms themselves.

The Marcel is a hotel small enough to provide an exclusive, intimate ambience, but big enough to offer all the services and technology business travelers need. Its character and size are shaped by its location, the heart of Manhattan, in one of the Big Apple's most bustling sections. It is a stone's throw from the shops of Fifth Avenue, Union Square, Greenwich Village, and the cultural offerings of midtown.

The fine materials used in the interior result in a neutral, restrained space. The décor plays with different textures in the same color range, from sand and beige to deep brown, to create a sense of continuity all the way from the building's entrance to the interiors of the rooms.

Several designers and modern artists collaborated to create a specific ambience. The lobby, designed by Malcolm Hill and John Paul Phillipe, is lined with horizontal teak panels. This creates an interesting texture that contrasts with the direction of the wood's grain. The furniture, designed by Eero Saarinen and Florence Knoll, is based on simple lines and rich materials, such as leather and velvet. Karim Rashid is the creative force behind the lighting, the business center, and the reading room. The overall effect of the mix emphasizes the modern lines and the feeling of relaxation. Inside the rooms, the play of the furnishings – the armoires, the shelving and beds that appear to be a single unit – the original artwork, and the huge windows overlooking Gramercy Park, all combine to create a striking atmosphere.

The Marcel

The combination of furniture styles, textures, and materials, such as leather, wood, and natural stone, create restrained, neutral spaces. Although there are some references to the style of the 1950s and 1960s, the overall effect is sober and tranquil.

The rooms are enriched with a wide variety of elements and materials such as leather headboards, built-in wooden shelves and armoires, and Belgian linen sheets.

Architects: Goodman Charlton Inc.   Photographer: Michael Kleinberg   Address: 201 East 24th Street, New York, United States   Tel.: 212 696 3800

Fax: 212 696 0077 www.nychotels.com Opening date: 1992 Number of rooms: 97 Services: restaurant, bar, terrace with view, reading room, video library, conference room

The Bentley, a luxurious Manhattan hotel, occupies a former office building. In 1998, after major renovations, it reopened its doors as a boutique hotel in one of the most exclusive parts of the city. The Upper East Side is home to such New York icons as Bloomingdales, the boutiques of the most famous designers, Fifth Avenue's Museum Mile, and some of the most luxurious residences in New York. Although the rooms are on the small side, an elegant and sophisticated ambience was achieved with a minimalist approach.

The project incorporates work by acclaimed designers such as Tom Baril, Ingo Maurer, and Malcolm Hill in a setting that includes basic materials and finishes with details of dark mahogany and stainless steel. The lobby combines materials such as sand and dark brown leather upholstery, light-colored silk draperies, and high ceilings with silver-colored circular lights. The contrast of light and dark tones accents the elegance of the hotel's public areas.

The rooms have a warmer, cozier feel, employing less formal furnishings, wood, and earth colors, ochre, and gold. The crowning touch is provided by the spectacular views of the northern part of Manhattan Island, the East River, and the Fifty-Ninth Street Bridge from many parts of the hotel, including the rooms.

The
Bentley

The panoramic views complement both the bar-restaurant and the rooms, providing a sense of spaciousness and adding a decorative touch.

Restrained lines are also employed in the rooms. The rich mix of materials and textures includes wood, wool carpets, parchment lamps, and linen sheets.

Architects: Goodman Charlton Inc.   Photographer: Michael Kleinberg   Address: 500 East 62nd Street, Nueva York, United States   Tel.: 212 644 6000   Fax: 212 207 4800

www.nychotels.com   Opening date: 1998   Number of rooms: 197 (includes 36 suites)   Services: terrace with view, parking, reading room, and library

The character of the former headquarters of the Chemists' Club, installed in this building in the mid-nineteenth century, is reflected throughout the hotel. The project, which accommodated the building to new needs, respected the original style of the structure in the façade, the public areas, and in rooms and most private spaces. Its location, in midtown Manhattan, is just steps from many points of interest for the wide range of tourists who visit New York. The interior design respected the decorative elements of the original space, and also departed from them to include new pieces. The furnishings and decorative objects are austere. A detailed study was carried out to find the palette most suitable to the character of the space. The cream and mauve which dominate the walls, the deep amethyst of the carpets, and the mahogany furnishings designed especially for the hotel create a peaceful, comfortable ambience.

From the entrance, the visitor's eye is drawn to the two-story hall that was once the ballroom of the Chemists' Club and is now, after the renovation that transformed it into the Dylan, the Virot Restaurant - which is open to the public. The space, dominated by the huge limestone fireplace, nearly two meters high, retains the plaster detail work on the false ceilings and the capitals of the columns, the flooring, and the woodwork. The bronze and alabaster lamps cast a subtle ambient light while creating a dialogue with the columns and original details, and the furniture, in mahogany or upholstered in dark tones, fades into the background.

Dylan
Hotel

The lighting and decorative details are designed along the same austere lines as the rest of the hotel. The low furniture, counters, and woodwork, in dark colors, contrast with the light, luminous tones of the lamps, walls, and drapes.

The size of the rooms makes it possible to include different ambiences in the same very bright space.

The view from the restaurant's balcony is dominated by the limestone fireplace. The restaurant
is the former Chemists' Club ballroom.

Architect: **M. Castedo**   Interior designer: **Jeffrey Beers International**   Photographer: **Jordi Miralles**   Address: **52 East 41 Street, New York, United States**   Tel./Fax: **212 338 0500**

Opening date: **1996**   Number of rooms: **108**   Services: **restaurant, data ports, gym, non-smoking floors**

The wall-mounted upholstered headboard and the cantilevered nightstands on either side of the bed, which serve as extra tables, add a touch of lightness to the room.

The bathrooms faced with white Carrara marble create a sophisticated ambience supported by the interior details. The porcelain bowl-shaped sinks resting on multi-colored granite slabs and the spigots built into the wall are reminiscent of the 1930s.

The Alchemy Suite is a room designed in 1932 as a replica of a chemical laboratory. It reproduces all the details of the neo-Gothic style which is so much a part of Manhattan.

The latest hotel opened in New York by the W Hotel chain combines the sense of history of a typical Manhattan neighborhood with the latest in business service technology. A contemporary design that contrasts dramatically with the existing structure reinforces this dialogue between the traditional and avant-garde. The hotel occupies the former Guardian Life building, a New York icon which is part of the urban landscape of Union Square. This is the first hotel to be established in this area, known traditionally for its exclusive restaurants and bars, shops featuring major designers, and the historic buildings on the Square. Now, after the area's renaissance, there are also tempting cultural offerings and a larger, more varied selection of shops and restaurants.

The entrances and special event spaces are arranged to create an easy, comfortable flow of traffic between the ceremonial areas, party or cocktail areas, and the spots reserved for more intimate, relaxed, sit-down dining. The Gathering Place is a light-filled space that brings to mind the early decades of the twentieth century, combining a bohemian opulence with the most refined style. The Grand Salon, a 2690 square feet hall that accommodates up to 180 for dinner and dancing, has retained the original marble columns and the wall decorations, which date back to 1911. The ceremonial nature of the space is broken by the arched windows, which afford excellent views of Union Square.

Modern services and high-tech capabilities make the hotel an attractive choice for business travelers. Every room has a high-speed data port, two telephone lines, remote control, and remote keyboards in a comfortable setting where every detail of color and texture has been carefully thought out. The choice of materials and colors enhances the features of the original structure. In the public areas, the light wood, the drapes, and the pale colors contrast with the tiles and the marble or stone detailing. The new look of this historic twenty-story building, retaining its emblematic aesthetic values and incorporating high-tech services, makes the hotel a new symbol of the urban recovery of this Manhattan neighborhood.

W NY
Union Square

The lobby is a two-story space flooded with light, where interior and exterior are closely related. The monumental nature of the space, which is the result of the proportions and some existing materials, is in contrast to the casual, almost informal furnishings, and the combination produces a unique atmosphere. The relationship of this space to the reception area is marked by drapes that surround the existing columns and act as sources of warm light.

The geometrical shapes of the reception area furnishings were inspired by the details of certain niches inside the building. Color differences supply contrast.

Architect: **David Rockwell**   Photographer: **Jordi Miralles**   Address: **201 Park Avenue, New York, United States**   Tel.: **212 2539119**   Fax: **212 253 9229**   **www.whotels.com**

Opening date: **November 2000**   Number of rooms: **270 (including 16 luxury suites)**   Services: **restaurant, bar, gym, library, high-tech business services, high-speed data ports, 24-hour room service**

The play of textures creates different niches in the main dining room while the lighting, colors, and furnishings provide a sense of unity.

Following page: The preexisting columns are prominent in the main area of the restaurant. These were the inspiration for the composition of the false ceilings, which create a more dynamic space.

Textures play an essential role in the rooms as well as in the public areas. In the lobby and the bar, the points of color created by the mosaic or the existing pieces of glass highlight certain features, such as the bar or views of Union Square. The walls' austere color and texture contrast with the richness of the natural fibers on the bed and elsewhere in the rooms' interiors.

A subtle play of transparencies and floral motifs repeated on the tables and the glass partitions creates a tranquil, peaceful atmosphere in the main dining room.